FIRST LADIES
FASCINATING FACTS

Diana Zourelias

Dover Publications, Inc.

Mineola, New York

NOTE

This book contains forty-six ready-to-color illustrations of all the First Ladies of the United States, from Martha Washington to Michelle Obama. These unique portraits were created by artist Diana Zourelias and they each highlight some unusual aspect of a First Lady's life or career. Plus, each page contains an interesting and informative caption filled with facts about one of America's First Ladies.

Bibliographical Note

First Ladies Fascinating Facts is a new work, first published by Dover Publications, Inc., in 2012.

International Standard Book Number
ISBN-13: 978-0-486-49832-4
ISBN-10: 0-486-49832-8

Manufactured in the United States by Courier Corporation
49832804   2015
www.doverpublications.com

Martha Washington

Martha Washington was our very first First Lady (although the term wasn't used at that time) from 1789 to 1797. She and George lived in a presidential mansion in New York City and then Philadelphia, which was the nation's capital while the Federal City (now Washington, D. C.) was under construction. Martha was beloved by Revolutionary War veterans for her support of the troops. During the war she had nursed the sick and wounded soldiers, repaired their uniforms and even darned their socks. In 1901, Martha became the first woman whose image was on a US postage stamp.

Abigail Adams

Abigail and John Adams were the first First Family to move into the President's House (the original name for the White House) in Washington, D.C., during the last year of his only term as president (1797-1801). Since construction wasn't completed on the mansion, it was cold and damp during the few months they lived there. Abigail used what is now the East Room as a drying room for the laundry—complete with a clothesline! The wife of the second president was also the mother of the sixth president, John Quincy Adams.

Martha "Patsy" Jefferson Randolph

Martha Wayles Skelton Jefferson died 19 years before her husband Thomas Jefferson became President. There is little description of Mrs. Jefferson and no known portrait of her other than one silhouette. However, it was known that during their marriage the couple enjoyed playing music for small gatherings that often included eldest daughter Martha (Patsy) in the audience. Patsy served as hostess during two winters (1802 and 1806) of her father's term of office.

Dolley Madison

Before the British invasion of Washington, D.C. during the War of 1812, James Madison's wife Dolley famously saved such valuables as a painting of George Washington, presidential papers, books, silver, china, draperies, and even her pet parrot from being destroyed by fire that swept through the White House. Serving from 1809 to 1817, Dolley was very popular and is the only First Lady to be given an honorary seat on the floor of Congress.

Elizabeth Monroe

As the wife of James Monroe, then the American Minister to France, Elizabeth Monroe visited the imprisoned wife of the Marquis de Lafayette in Paris. After news spread of Mrs. Monroe's visit, the French government released Adrienne de Lafayette as a gesture of good will toward their U.S. ally. During her years as First Lady, from 1817 to 1825, Elizabeth suffered from poor health and made few public appearances.

Louisa Adams

Louisa Adams was the only First Lady born in another country—England. An accomplished musician, she loved to play the harp. She also composed music and wrote poetry, essays and plays. Mrs. Adams is also remembered for raising silk worms in the mulberry trees at the White House. She was First Lady from 1825 to 1829.

Emily Donelson
Niece

Sarah Yorke Jackson
Daughter-In-Law

Rachel Jackson
Emily Donelson/Sarah Yorke Jackson

The happy marriage of Rachel and Andrew Jackson was marred by scandal about Rachel's first marriage. The gossip threatened to ruin her husband's political career and strained Rachel's physical and mental health. Sadly, she died of a heart attack in December 1828, just weeks before her husband's inauguration, never serving as First Lady. Niece Emily Donelson and daughter-in-law Sarah Yorke Jackson both served as hostesses during Jackson's term (1829 to 1837), the only time two women served simultaneously as "First Lady."

Angelica Singleton Van Buren

Martin Van Buren's beloved wife Hannah died of tuberculosis at the age of 35—18 years before he became president. For the first half of his presidency, the widowed Van Buren had no official hostess. However, after the marriage of his oldest son Abraham to 22-year-old Angelica Singleton in 1838, the president asked his new daughter-in-law to serve as First Lady (1838–1841). The daughter of a South Carolina planter and a cousin of the former first lady Dolley Madison, Angelica created a welcome tie between the northern White House politicians and Southern society.

Anna Harrison

Anna Harrison was First Lady for only one month in 1841 and never had the privilege of living in the White House. In fact, when her husband, William Henry Harrison, died of pneumonia only 31 days after taking office, Anna was still home packing for her move to the capital city. She had ten children, the most ever by a first lady, and helped raise her grandson Benjamin, who would one day become the 23rd president of the United States.

Letitia Tyler

Letitia Tyler was First Lady for less than a year and a half. Having suffered a stroke the year before her husband John became vice president, she was still in poor health when he succeeded to the presidency following the death of William Henry Harrison on April 4, 1841. Although she spent a great deal of time in her room, the mother of seven managed to keep up with the activities of her children and growing number of grandchildren. Letitia died in September 1842, the first of three First Ladies who died in the White House. Daughter-in-law Priscilla Cooper Tyler served as official hostess from 1841 to 1843. Daughter Letita "Letty" Tyler Semple served briefly as hostess in 1844.

Julia Gardiner Tyler

John Tyler's second wife, Julia, was the second youngest presidential wife to serve as First Lady (24 years old) and the one with the shortest tenure, only eight months—June 1844 to March 1845. But she made history during her brief stay in the White House. In addition to being the first First Lady to sit for a photograph, she was also the first First Lady to dance publicly during her tenure. Near the end of the Tyler administration she hosted a "Grand Finale Ball" for 3,000 invited guests!

Sarah Polk

Intelligent, witty, and very religious, Sarah Polk was a popular First Lady who devoted all of her time to her husband's career. She thought dancing was improper in the President's house and banned it, along with hard liquor and card playing. However, she did request that "Hail to the Chief" be played whenever the president entered a room in order to draw attention to the rather diminutive James Polk. She was First Lady from 1845 to 1849.

Margaret (Peggy) Taylor
Betty Taylor Bliss

Peggy Taylor, a military wife in the years prior to moving to the White House, was more comfortable supervising the household maintenance than presiding over public functions as First Lady. So she happily assigned the duties of official hostess to her popular young daughter, Mary Elizabeth "Betty" Taylor Bliss. Unfortunately, their time in the Washington was brief; Zachary Taylor died in office on July 9, 1850, after only eighteen months as president.

Abigail Fillmore

Abigail Fillmore worked as a public schoolteacher before and after her marriage to Millard Fillmore, making her the first First Lady to have had a paying job as a married woman. A lifelong lover of books, she and her husband built a personal library of over four thousand titles and she is credited with decorating and expanding the official White House library during her tenure. She served as First Lady from 1850 to 1853 and died just a few weeks after her husband left office.

Jane Pierce

Shy and reclusive Jane Pierce actually fainted when her husband, Franklin, was nominated for president. Prone to depression following the tragic and untimely deaths of her three children, Jane's years as First Lady (1853 to 1857) were difficult. She did, however, oversee some decorative changes to the White House, including the addition of a furnace, a tile-covered bathroom with hot and cold running water, ornate mirrors and a beautiful set of china purchased at the New York World's Fair.

Harriet Lane

Young and beautiful Harriet Lane was raised by her uncle James Buchanan, the only bachelor President. She served as his First Lady from 1857 to 1861. In 1860, Harriet charmed the Prince of Wales (later King Edward VII), the first member of the British royal family to visit the US. The press followed them as they toured Mount Vernon, danced together and even played a game of tenpins. Harriet donated her invaluable art collection to the Smithsonian as well as a generous sum of money for a pediatric facility at Johns Hopkins Hospital.

Mary Todd Lincoln

When her husband Abraham was elected President, the politically active and socially ambitious Mary Todd Lincoln was thrilled. As First Lady she worked as a volunteer nurse and supported efforts to abolish slavery. In fact, her 1861 inaugural ball gown was created by seamstress Elizabeth Keckley, a freed slave who became Mary's close friend and confidant. But her years in the White House (1861-1865) were difficult and filled with tragedy—the trauma of the Civil War, the sudden death of her son Willie, and the assassination of her husband as she sat beside him. She passed away in 1882, a tragic and misunderstood figure in American history.

Eliza Johnson

Eliza Johnson is credited with being a tremendous support to her husband Andrew, helping him hone his public speaking and debating skills. Moving into the White House following the assassination of Abraham Lincoln was a difficult time for the Johnsons. Due to her frail health during her years as First Lady (1865-1869), Eliza limited her duties to hosting formal White House dinners. Her daughter Martha Patterson assumed primary hostess responsibilities, often aided by her sister Mary Stover.

Julia Dent Grant

The wife of wartime hero Ulysses S. Grant, Julia was a cheerful source of strength for her husband. Moving into the White House after the horrors of the Civil War years, she transformed the shabby mansion into an elegant and welcoming home during their tenure from 1869 to 1877. Julia loved being First Lady and referred to her years in the White House as "the happiest period" of her life. And, despite having a "lazy" eye (thus always photographed in profile), Julia was adventurous and determined—even agreeing to descend into the gloomy depths of silver mine when she learned that her husband had bet she would be too afraid to go!

19

Lucy Hayes

With a liberal arts degree from Cincinnati Wesleyan Female College, Lucy Hayes was the first First Lady to graduate with a higher education degree. Known for her strong religious and moral beliefs, she supported her husband Rutherford's ban of all alcoholic beverages from the White House, earning her the nickname "Lemonade Lucy." Under the direction of Mrs. Hayes, the tradition of the White House Easter egg roll was born and continues to this day. It was during her tenure (1877-1881) that the term "First Lady" became popular nationwide.

Lucretia Garfield

Lucretia Garfield was a college graduate and worked as an art teacher before marrying James Garfield in 1858. She was a reserved woman who exhibited calm, courage, and strength—qualities that served her well after the shooting and eventual death of her husband in 1881. "Crete," as she was known, was First Lady for only a little over six months, the second shortest tenure in history. She was one of the first presidential candidate's wives to appear on a campaign poster.

Mary "Molly" Arthur McElroy

Ellen Arthur, the wife of Chester Arthur, died suddenly in early 1880, ten months before her husband was elected vice president. When Chester assumed the presidency in September of 1881 after Garfield's death, he was still mourning the loss of his wife. He paid for the installation of a memorial stained glass window in a church visible from his private White House residence, where a portrait of Ellen was on display. Mary Arthur McElroy, the President's sister, acted as First Lady from 1883 to 1885.

Frances Cleveland

Frances Cleveland was the first woman to become First Lady by marrying a sitting president. At age 21, she was also the youngest presidential wife to become a First Lady. The historic wedding of the only President and First Lady to wed in the White House attracted worldwide attention. Forty-nine-year-old Grover Cleveland was a law partner of Frances' late father and had known his future bride her entire life. She served as First Lady from 1886 to 1889.

Caroline Harrison

Caroline Harrison brought a flair for music, art and design to the White House. She was also ahead of her time in many of the women's causes that she championed including the use of American goods and the admittance of women to medical school. As First Lady from 1889 until her death in 1892, she had electricity installed in the White House and made china painting popular. Her hobby led her to catalog past administration's china and to design her own White House dishes using a motif that included ears of corn and the goldenrod.

Frances Cleveland

Frances Cleveland returned to the White House with her husband Grover in 1893 after a four-year absence and saw her popularity continue to grow. In September 1893 the First Family welcomed the addition of a second child they named Esther. This was the first and only time a First Lady gave birth to a child in the White House. People were so excited about the new baby that the First Family was forced to close the mansion to the public because of safety concerns.

Ida McKinley

Ida McKinley was the only First Lady to have worked as a bank teller and manager. Physically and emotionally fragile during her years in the White House (1897-1901), she relied completely on her husband William. The vice-president's wife Jennie Hobart helped her with hostess duties. Often confined to her private quarters, Ida spent the time knitting hundreds of bedroom slippers that would be auctioned off for large sums of money, which was donated to local and national charities.

Edith Roosevelt

Edith was a childhood friend of Theodore Roosevelt's and married him after the death of his first wife. Her cool, even temperament was seen as the perfect balance to her excitable, adventurous husband. As First Lady from 1901 to 1909, Edith made a great impact on the position. She restored the White House to its 18th Century style, added a West Wing, established the First Ladies' Gallery, started a permanent china collection and hired the first social secretary, which gave her more time to care for the six Roosevelt children.

Helen Taft

Helen "Nellie" Taft, wife of William Howard Taft, accomplished many firsts as First Lady. She was the first First Lady to own and drive a car, the first to ride in her husband's inaugural parade, the first to support women's suffrage, the first to publish her memoirs, the first to smoke cigarettes, and the first to successfully lobby for safety standards in federal workplaces. She was also responsible for the planting of the famous Japanese cherry blossom trees in Washington D.C. as well as establishing free public concerts in West Potomac Park. She served as First Lady from 1909–1913.

ELLEN AXSON
WILSON

View of the Griswold
House Back Porch

Ellen Wilson

Georgia-born Ellen Wilson was a talented painter and remains the only professional artist to serve as First Lady. Although devoted to her husband Woodrow and his political career, Ellen pursued her own interests during her brief time as First Lady— she painted in her studio; oversaw the creation of the Rose Garden; and campaigned for better housing for Washington's poor and for stricter child labor laws. Unfortunately, she died of kidney disease in August 1914 after almost a year and a half in the White House.

Edith Wilson

Edith Wilson, Woodrow Wilson's second wife, was one of the most influential First Ladies in American history. Married on December 18, 1915, she immediately became her husband's most trusted advisor and confidante. When the President suffered a debilitating stroke in October of 1919, Edith guarded access to him from advisors and other political figures and kept the seriousness of his illness a secret for weeks. Although she never made any major decisions, legend has labeled her the "Secret President." She served as First Lady from 1915–1921.

Florence Kling Harding

Warren G. Harding's wife, Florence, whom he affectionately called "the Duchess," was a very popular First Lady. She was very active in her husband's presidential campaign and he consulted with her on his political decisions. She used her time in the White House (1921-1923) to promote issues such as veteran's benefits, the protection of animals, and women's rights. Florence was the first First Lady to be assigned her own Secret Service agent. But, more importantly to her, she was the first First Lady to vote!

Grace Coolidge

Grace Coolidge attended the University of Vermont and later trained for teaching at the Clarke School for the Deaf in Northampton, MA. She was a charming, bright, and friendly person, the perfect counterpoint to her dour husband, Calvin. During her tenure as First Lady (1923-1929), Grace faithfully followed baseball, but never politics. Home and family were the center of her life. An animal lover, she kept a large variety of pets in the White House, including Rebecca the Raccoon and a white collie named Rob Roy.

Lou Hoover

Lou Hoover met Herbert Hoover while both were attending Stanford University. Mrs. Hoover led an extraordinarily active life before becoming First Lady, traveling all over the world with her husband and becoming fluent in five language, including Chinese! Very interested in the welfare of young people, she held various leadership positions in the Girls Scouts, which she helped create, acting as its Honorary President during her White House years from 1929 to 1933—every succeeding First Lady since Mrs. Hoover has assumed that role.

Eleanor Roosevelt

Eleanor Roosevelt dramatically changed the role of First Lady and is considered by many to be among the greatest of the women who have had that title. She held regular press conferences; wrote newspaper and magazine columns; and hosted a weekly radio show. Eleanor spoke out in behalf of human rights, women's issues, and children's causes. In 1939, as an advocate for civil rights, she arranged for African-American opera singer Marian Anderson to perform at the Lincoln Memorial after the Daughters of the American Revolution had refused the singer permission to appear at Constitution Hall. Eleanor served as First Lady from 1933 to 1945.

Elizabeth Virginia "Bess" Truman

Bess Truman was seen as shy and reserved and in her nearly eight years as First Lady she never held a press conference or gave an interview. But she did fulfill her social obligations and during her White House years (1945-1953) she shook so many hands that the glove size of her right hand went from 6 to 6 ½! Bess and husband Harry met as children at Sunday school and were devoted to one another throughout their lives. Harry relied on her greatly and told friends that he never made an important decision without first consulting his wife. Mrs. Truman was the longest living of the First Ladies; she died in 1982 at the age of 97.

Mamie Eisenhower

A charming and gracious hostess, Mamie Eisenhower was a popular First Lady famous for her bangs, sparkling blue eyes, pretty clothes and jewelry, and happy family life. She was not concerned with politics or causes and during her White House years (1953-1961) her priorities were her home and her husband. Her favorite color was pink and it showed up often in her wardrobe and in the décor of the family residence of the White House. She was a devoted fan of popular television comedy shows and soap operas and often watched them in her private quarters.

Jacqueline Kennedy

Attractive, intelligent, and fashionable, Jackie Kennedy was the first true celebrity First Lady and one of the most admired and respected women in the world. She met her future husband, John F. Kennedy, when he was a Congressman and she was working for the Washington Times-Herald as its Inquiring Camera Girl. As First Lady, Mrs. Kennedy went to great lengths to transform the White House into a museum of American history and culture and won an honorary Emmy award for her efforts. Just 31 years old when she became First Lady in 1961, tragically, she was only 34 years old when she was widowed following her husband's assassination in 1963.

Claudia "Lady Bird" Johnson

Lady Bird Johnson was thrust into the spotlight when she suddenly became First Lady after the assassination of President Kennedy in 1963. Two years later at her husband Lyndon's inaugural ceremony, she was the first First Lady to hold the bible as he took the presidential oath. Every First Lady since then has followed this custom. During her years at the White House (1963-1969) Mrs. Johnson's spent a tremendous amount of time and effort trying to conserve our nation's natural resources through her "Beautification" program. This included anti-pollution measures, water and air reclamation, landscaping and urban renewal plans.

Thelma Catherine "Pat" Nixon

Pat Nixon, the first First Lady to appear publicly in pants, served from 1969 to 1974, the year her husband Richard became the first and only U.S. President to resign from office. In happier times, Mrs. Nixon used her popularity to encourage volunteer service and to endorse the Equal Rights Amendment. Until Hillary Clinton, Pat held the record as the most-traveled First Lady. She toured as a goodwill ambassador, met with political leaders, and led major humanitarian efforts in many different countries. After her famous visit to China, two Giant Pandas were sent to the National Zoo in Washington as gifts to the U.S.

Betty Ford

Betty Ford became First Lady after President Nixon resigned in 1974, making her husband, Vice President Gerald Ford, the 38th President. She became known and admired for being unusually frank and candid about serious and personal subjects, openly discussing her battle with breast cancer. Years later, as a former First Lady, she helped establish the Betty Ford Center, dedicated to helping people with chemical dependency. A trained dancer, Betty famously danced atop the Cabinet Room table in the final days of her husband's administration in 1977.

Rosalynn Carter

Politically active Rosalynn Carter broke new ground as First Lady, serving openly as her husband's advisor during their White House years (1977-1981). The hardworking Mrs. Carter was the first First Lady to have an office in the East Wing and attend Cabinet meetings and major briefings. In her role as First Lady she focused national attention on the performing arts and supported programs focusing on mental health and the elderly. Rosalynn and Jimmy Carter, along with their children, were the first First Family to walk the parade route from the Capitol to the White House on Inauguration Day.

Nancy Reagan

Nancy Reagan was originally a Hollywood actress and appeared in eleven feature films. In her last movie, *Hellcats of the Navy,* she costarred with her husband, the actor and future president Ronald Reagan. The fashionable Nancy brought glamour back to the White House and hosted over 56 state dinners during her tenure (1981-1989). However, her primary project as First Lady was the creation of the "Just Say No" nationwide campaign, funding drug education and prevention programs for children and young adults.

Barbara Bush

Like Abigail Adams, Barbara Bush was the wife and mother of presidents and very popular for her motherly, down-to-earth manner. With a love of reading encouraged early on, she focused her efforts as First Lady (1989-1993) on bringing national attention and financial support to illiteracy in America, creating the Barbara Bush Foundation for Family Literacy. Famous for her affection for her pet dog Millie, an English springer spaniel, she was understandably proud of the best-selling *Millie's Book,* as dictated to Barbara Bush.

Hillary Rodham Clinton

Hillary Rodham Clinton, a lawyer and one of the most political of all First Ladies, played a very active role in her husband Bill's administration (1993-2001). She helped raise the national consciousness about the problems of citizens without medical insurance and was successful in initiating the Children's Health Insurance Program. On November 7, 2000, Mrs. Clinton became the first First Lady ever elected to public office, winning a Senate seat from New York. In 2007 she announced her candidacy for president. Although she lost the nomination, she received more votes than any previous woman candidate. In 2008 President Barack Obama named her Secretary of State.

Laura Bush

A former teacher and librarian, Laura Bush was one of the most popular first ladies and dedicated her years in the White House (2001-2009) to raising awareness and support for literacy around the globe. She founded the annual National Book Festival and launched "Ready to Read, Ready to Learn" to promote early childhood education. As Ambassador for the National Heart, Lung, and Blood Institute's Heart Truth campaign, Mrs. Bush traveled extensively to educate women about the symptoms of heart disease, the number one killer of American women. Laura and George W. Bush are the only presidential couple to be parents of twins. (Interestingly, no U.S. President has been a twin.)

Michelle Obama

The wife of Barack Obama, the first African-American U.S. President, Michelle worked as a lawyer, Chicago city administrator and community outreach worker before taking on the role of First Lady in 2009. Since then she has focused her attention on issues such as the support of military families, helping working women balance career and family, stressing the importance of education and volunteer work and fighting childhood obesity. Mrs. Obama worked with local school children to plant a 1,100 square foot garden of fresh vegetables on the South Lawn of the White House.